British Sports
For The Amusement Of Children

William Belch

Alpha Editions

This Edition Published in 2021

ISBN: 9789354417627

Design and Setting By
Alpha Editions
www.alphaedis.com
Email – info@alphaedis.com

As per information held with us this book is in Public Domain. This book is a reproduction of an important historical work. Alpha Editions uses the best technology to reproduce historical work in the same manner it was first published to preserve its original nature. Any marks or number seen are left intentionally to preserve its true form.

's

EDITIONS OF
CHILDREN's BOOKS.

PRICE 6d. COLOURED.

Entertaining Views
Scenes from Nature
Rural Scenes
Youthful Sports
Birds
Beasts
Fishes and Insects
Fruit and Flowers
Alphabet of Nations
British Sports
Foreign Sports
Capitals of Europe
Nursery Calculations, or a
Peep into Numbers.

1s. & 1s. 6d. CHILDREN's BOOKS, Plain and Coloured.

PLAIN & COLOURED LOTTERIES,
very great Variety.

6d. 9d. 1s. and 1s. 3d. DRAWING BOOKS, Plain and Coloured.

BRITISH SPORTS, for the Amusement of CHILDREN

PHEASANT SHOOTING.

See the Fowler takes his aim,
To bring down the feather'd game;
September Season is the time,
When these birds are in full prime.

LONDON.
Printed, Published & Sold by
W. Belch, Newington Butts.

RABBIT SHOOTING.

How happy & frisky the Rabbits appear,
Prancing & skipping without any fear;
But alas, their enjoyment is like to be short,
By the aim of a Gunner who seeks them for sport

BADGER BAITING.

Baited by Dogs, the Badger dies,
A cruel sport it thus supplies,
The Skin is by the Furriers bought,
And thus for gain & pleasure sought.

HORSE RACING.

Goaded with Spurs they seem to fly,
Like lightning to the human eye,
Stretch out their necks to gain the post
While thousands on the course are lost

STAG HUNT.

The timid Stag with eager bounds,
Strives to escape pursuing Hounds;
In vain he flies he's doom'd to die,
Whilst shouts of Huntsmen rend the Sky.

COURSING.

They beat the Bush to find a Hare,
And thus for a long chace prepare;
Poor gentle Puss thy fate is hard,
And it with pity I regard.

FOX CHACE.

The Fox is Reynard sly and cunning,
Often with our Poultry running;
To hunt him yields a manly sport,
And numbers to the chace resort.

ANGLING.

Angling will oft our patience try,
Ere we a dish of Fish supply;
Yet many love the rural sport,
And to the Brook or Lake resort.

SCHOOL PIECES,
(IN VERY GREAT VARIETY)
with
THREE WHOLE-SHEET FLOURISHING DITTO,
Plain and Coloured.

Isaiah
Jehu
Isaac and Rebekah
Samuel and Saul
Queen Elizabeth
Christ's Sermon on the Mount
Nathan's Parable
Life of Saint Paul
Miraculous Draught of Fishes
Jeptha's Rash Vow
Whittington and his Cat
Coronation
Life of Christ
Life of Joshua
Life of Solomon
Life of Moses
Life of Joseph
Life of Job
Life of Jonah
Life of Pharoah
Life of Abraham
Acts of the Apostles
Adam and Eve
Deserted Village
Pope's Prayer
Pilgrim's Progress
Lord's Prayer
Ten Commandments
Apostles' Creed

Naaman cured of his Leprosy
Creation of the World
Morning Hymn
Evening Hymn
Revelation of St. John
Queen Sheba's Visit to King Solomon
Noah's Ark
David and Goliah
Daniel in the Lion's Den
Robinson Crusoe
King Alfred
Beggar's Petition
Chevy Chase
Economy of Human Life
Seven Wonders of the World
Conversion of St. Paul
Captain Cook
Horse Soldiers
Balloon
God save the King
Rule Britannia
Edward the Black Prince
Death of Ananias
Pharisee and Publican
Three Warnings
End of Time.

With additional new ones annually.

SLIP COPIES, BLACK LINES, MAP FILES, AND
FLOURISHING SCHOOL-PIECE BOOKS.

www.ingramcontent.com/pod-product-compliance
Lightning Source LLC
Chambersburg PA
CBHW030711110426
42739CB00031B/1801